THE WORLD OF

Mathematics
Revision

Andy Ballard

Contents

Page

Magic squares

Izzy is collecting old newspapers and magazines for recycling. As she puts them into a pile, the puzzle page in one magazine catches her eye. She tries a brainteaser called The Magic Square. This is what it looks like.

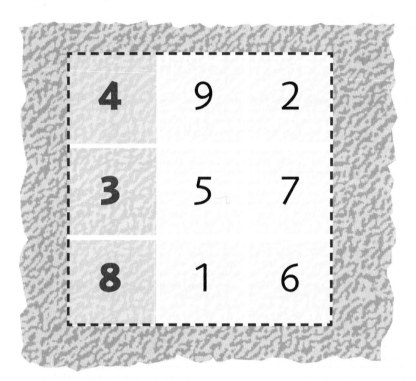

At first, Izzy can't see what is magic about the numbers so she adds the digits in the first column **4 + 3 + 8**. They total 15. She notices that the numbers in the first row, 4 + 9 + 2, also add up to 15. Then she tries making the totals of the other columns and rows. Each one makes 15.

Next she tries the diagonals. Amazingly, they total 15 too.

Now she can see why it is called a magic square. All the numbers in each row, column and <u>diagonal</u> add up to the same total.

Hidden numbers

A dog has walked muddy paw prints all over these sums. What are the missing numbers?

1 6 + ⬤ + 7 = 15

2 10 − ⬤ − 4 = 4

3 −2 + ⬤ + 1 = 4

4 5 + 1 − 3 = ⬤

Could it be magic?

Here is another magic square. Can you work out what each row, column and diagonal should add up to? Now complete the square.

−2	*	*
5	1	−3
*	*	4

• TOP TIPS •

Adding several numbers together is easy if you do two at a time, especially if some are negative.

DID YOU KNOW?

−3 + 5 = +2   +3 − 5 = −2

If you add a <u>positive</u> number to a negative number you don't automatically know if your answer will be positive or negative! It depends on the size of the two numbers you're adding.

Think of a number

Izzy's dad, Ralph, is always looking for new ways to challenge his daughter. Today he has a maths game. He thinks of a number and changes it in some way. He tells her how and then tells her the number he ends up with. Izzy has to work out the number he first thought of. She's allowed a pen and paper if she wants them.

'Here's your first one,' announces Ralph. 'I'm thinking of a number. I've doubled it. My answer is 16. What number did I start with?'

After a little thought, and checking her answer is 16 when doubled, Izzy says, 'The number you originally thought of was 8.'

Ralph is amazed so he sets her a few more to try.

1   I think of a number. I add 1. Then I multiply by 2. My answer is 8.

2   I think of a number. I multiply by 3. Then I add 4. I get 19.

3   I think of a number. I <u>square</u> it. My answer is 16.

4   I think of a number. I divide it by 2. Then I add 1. I get 8.

5   I think of a number. I subtract 5. Then I divide by 3. I get 8.

The answers are 3, 5, 4, 14 and 29.

Izzy has been quietly turning each question into an <u>equation</u> because it's easier to write down than all those words.

For Ralph's original question, Izzy wrote $2r = 16$.
(*r* is the number **R**alph thought of)

What's the letter?

Work out the value of the letter in each of these equations.

1 $3r = 12$

2 $2a - 5 = 15$

3 $2(b + 3) = 8$

4 $\dfrac{x}{8} = 3$

5 $3(y + 5) = 12$

6 $c^2 + 5 = 30$

· TOP TIPS ·

To make them easier to solve, each of the questions on the previous page can be written down as an equation.

1 $2(r + 1) = 8$ $r = 3$

2 $3r + 4 = 19$ $r = 5$

3 $r^2 = 16$ $r = 4$

4 $\dfrac{r}{2} + 1 = 8$ $r = 14$

5 $\dfrac{(r - 5)}{3} = 8$ $r = 29$

DID YOU KNOW?

The square of 3 is 9. The square root of 9 is not just 3!

There are two numbers that, when squared, give an answer of 9. They are 3 and –3 ($-3 \times -3 = +9$).

So the square root of 9 is actually '3 or –3'.

In the old days

Ralph has been showing Izzy his old maths exercise book from his school days. There are hundreds of questions on fractions and decimals but Ralph has forgotten how he did them all. And he never did understand percentages.

Izzy sets about figuring it all out. She writes down what she knows about changing numbers from fractions to decimals and from decimals to percentages.

Fraction to decimal

Top ÷ Bottom

e.g. $\frac{3}{4} = 3 \div 4 = 0.75$

Decimal to %

× 100%

e.g. $0.75 = 0.75 \times 100\% = 75\%$

On one of the exercise book pages, there is a really clever way of comparing fractions.

The steeper the line, the larger the fraction!

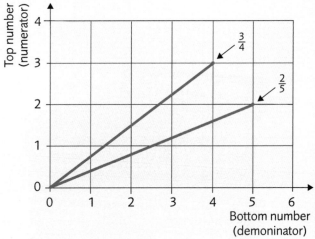

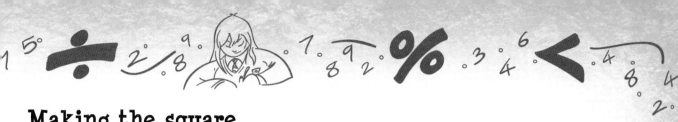

Making the square

The dominoes below have to be arranged into the <u>square</u> shown. Two have been done for you. Can you fill in the rest?

If D is a decimal, and P is a percentage, what should they be?

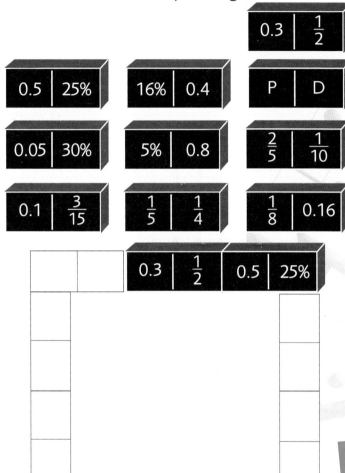

| 0.3 | $\frac{1}{2}$ |

| 0.5 | 25% | | 16% | 0.4 | | P | D |

| 0.05 | 30% | | 5% | 0.8 | | $\frac{2}{5}$ | $\frac{1}{10}$ |

| 0.1 | $\frac{3}{15}$ | | $\frac{1}{5}$ | $\frac{1}{4}$ | | $\frac{1}{8}$ | 0.16 |

| 0.3 | $\frac{1}{2}$ | 0.5 | 25% |

DID YOU KNOW?

The symbol > means greater than and < means less than.

So 3 < 5 and 4 > –2.

Also $\frac{3}{4} > \frac{2}{5}$.

• TOP TIPS •

Decimal to fraction is harder.

Put the decimal out of 100ths first, then cancel down if you can.

e.g. $0.2 = 0.20 = \frac{20}{100} = \frac{1}{5}$

e.g. $0.15 = \frac{15}{100} = \frac{3}{20}$

e.g. $0.04 = \frac{4}{100} = \frac{1}{25}$

Test your knowledge 1

1 a) Place the following numbers in order, smallest to largest. **(2 marks)**

$$7 \qquad 2 \qquad -3 \qquad -4 \qquad 5$$

b) Calculate:

   (i) $-5 + 8 =$ **(1 mark)**

   (ii) $8 - 5 =$ **(1 mark)**

   (iii) $3 - 6 + 4 =$ **(1 mark)**

   (iv) $9 - 5 - 6 =$ **(1 mark)**

2 Work out the following:

a) $4^2 =$ **(1 mark)**

b) $(5 + 6)^2 =$ **(2 marks)**

c) $3(2 + 1) =$ **(2 marks)**

d) $5(6 - 8) =$ **(2 marks)**

3 Solve each equation:

a) $4r = 12$ **(1 mark)**

b) $m^2 = 25$ **(2 marks)**

c) $3t - 2 = 16$ **(2 marks)**

d) $2(g + 2) = 12$ **(2 marks)**

4 Place in the correct order, smallest to largest.

a) 31%   13%   33%   3%   30%   **(2 marks)**

b) 0.32   0.123   0.03   0.23   0.02   **(2 marks)**

c) $\frac{1}{10}$ $\frac{2}{5}$ $\frac{5}{6}$ $\frac{2}{3}$ $\frac{1}{3}$ **(2 marks)**

d) $\frac{1}{3}$ 0.04   0.54 $\frac{1}{2}$ 45%   **(2 marks)**

5 Johnny thinks of a number, multiplies it by 3 and then subtracts 4.
In each case below, find the number Johnny thought of if the answer is:

a) 2   **(2 marks)**

b) 11   **(2 marks)**

c) −10   **(2 marks)**

6 Complete the table.   **(6 marks)**

Decimal	Fraction	Percentage
0.3		
		25%
	$\frac{3}{5}$	

(Total 40 marks)

Patio makeover

Ralph has asked Max to redesign the walled
garden. Max would like to create a new patio area.
He wants the flagstones to be in a pattern.

The thing is, he doesn't know what available space
there will be and wants a choice of patterns for the
flagstones. He knows he definitely doesn't want
wooden decking.

These are Max's first plans:

Pattern 1   **Pattern 2**   **Pattern 3**

When Max looked at the plans, he was able to make out patterns within the patterns.
He has spotted what is happening to individual colours and shading.

He filled in this table:

Colour	Pattern 1	Pattern 2	Pattern 3
Purple	1	1	1
Orange	4	8	12
Red	4	12	24
White	0	4	12

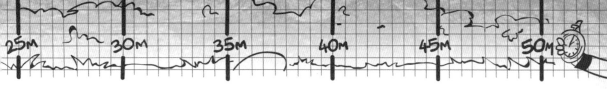

Expanding sequences

1 How many flagstones would there be of each colour if Max extended his plans to a fourth pattern? Sketch the pattern and fill in the table.

Colour	Pattern 4
Purple	
Orange	
Red	
White	

2 The first three patterns in an expanding sequence are shown.

N = 1

N = 2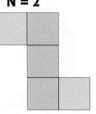

N = 3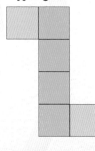

Complete this table.

Colour	N = 1	N = 2	N = 3	N = 4
Pink, p				
Yellow, y				

Write down an equation for each of p and y.

DID YOU KNOW?

Roman floors were often made of tiles. Different colours were used to make pictures, which are called mosaics.

• TOP TIPS •

Sometimes you can make an equation to work how many tiles there will be in each colour. In Max's patio patterns, if p is the pattern number (1, 2, 3) then Purple = 1 (as it's always 1) and Orange = 4p.

Code breaker

Ralph has decided to rebuild the walls in the walled garden from scratch. This means he can increase the size of the garden (and his patio!). The rose bed will be 3 metres wide and the remainder of the garden will be square.

The question he needs to answer is how long the walls will be for different sized gardens. Max has given Izzy a sketch and an equation for working out the <u>perimeter</u> of the garden. But can Izzy make sense of it?

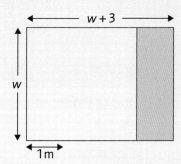

$P = 2(2w + 3) - 1$

The garden is $w + 3$ metres long and w metres wide.

As the garden is a <u>rectangle</u>, the two lengths and the two widths are the same. So the perimeter of the rectangle is $2(w + w + 3) = 4w + 6$. There's a gap in the wall of 1 m to be subtracted for a gate.

So if the garden width, w, is to be 10 m, then the perimeter can be worked out using the equation:

$$P = 4w + 6 - 1$$
$$= 4 \times 10 + 6 - 1$$
$$= 45\,\text{m}$$

> It's a rather simpler equation to use, don't you think...?

Max smiles smugly as he's worked out a simpler code (equation).

Just adding up the sides of the rectangle and subtracting the 1 m gives:

$$w + w + 3 + w + w + 3 - 1 = 4w + 5$$

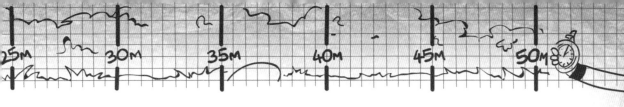

How many cards?

The children in two families send postcards to each other when they go on holiday. There are four sons in the Smith family and three daughters in the Jones family. Each son sends a card to each of the daughters. Each daughter sends a card to each son. The diagram shows this.

s = 4

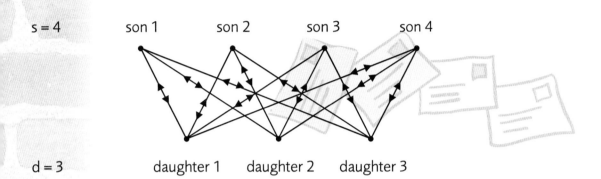

son 1   son 2   son 3   son 4

d = 3   daughter 1   daughter 2   daughter 3

a) How many cards are sent in total?

The number of cards sent can be found using the equation

$c = 2sd$

where s is the number of sons, and d is the number of daughters.

b) If there were 12 sons and 8 daughters, how many cards would be sent?

• TOP TIPS •

There are often several valid equations that suit a diagram or pattern. They are all <u>equivalent</u> and are simplifications of each other. Always find the simplest equation that you can, and look for ways to simplify it.

DID YOU KNOW?

Most postcards are rectangles. About 2,500 years ago the Greeks discovered the 'golden rectangle', which was thought to have an especially pleasing look. The longer side is about 1.62 times the length of the shorter side. You can probably find a postcard or some other rectangle that is close to being a golden rectangle.

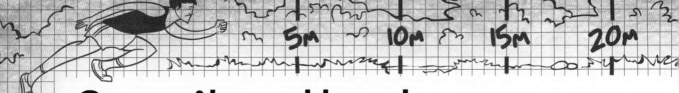

Opposites attract

Every year, Ralph hosts a charity banquet. The big event is next week and Ralph is trying to help Max plan the table. Ralph is worried about whether there will be enough cutlery. There are eight guests to seat and seven courses to serve. But how much cutlery will they need?

Ralph starts by trying to work out what eight sevens are, but he has never been any good at his seven times tables. Max has a possible solution: work out seven eights!

$$7 \times 8 = 56$$

Max has shown that 7×8 is the same as 8×7. Many maths problems can be solved in more than one way.

Another example is **5 + 6 is the same as 6 + 5**.

Working out **3 + 4 + 5 can be done as (3 + 4) + 5** doing the 3 + 4 bracket first, **or as 3 + (4 + 5)** doing 4 + 5 = 9 first.

The same applies for multiplications:

3.5 × 5 × 2 can be worked out as (3.5 × 5) × 2 or as 3.5 × (5 × 2).

The second way gives $3.5 \times 10 = 35$. You might think this is easier than doing it the first way.

Be careful though. 12 ÷ 3 is not the same as 3 ÷ 12.

Equations can be written in different ways too. For example, **$a + b = 6$ can be written as $a = 6 - b$**. It's still the same equation but looks different.

Whatever values a and b have in the first equation, the second equation will still be true. So, if $a = 2$ and $b = 4$ then the original equation works as $a + b = 2 + 4 = 6$. The new equation $a = 6 - b$ works as $2 = 6 - 4$.

Other ways are $b = 6 - a$ and $b + a = 6$. $6 = a + b$ is also true, but it's a 'reflection' of the original, so we'll ignore it. ($a + b - 6 = 0$ is another but there's a fourth <u>term</u>, the zero.)

These are all the ways of writing the equation using just the terms a, b and 6.

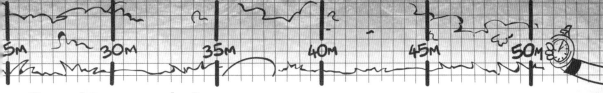

Equation match

Equations can be written in different ways. Match each of the equations A to E with one of the three equations in the box.

1 $e + f = 10$ **2** $e - f = 10$ **3** $e + 10 = f$

A: $f - e = 10$

B: $10 + f = e$

C: $e - 10 = f$

D: $e = 10 - f$

E: $f - 10 = e$

• TOP TIPS •

Putting numbers into your equations is a good way of checking your answers. Make sure you choose numbers that work in the original equation.

For example:

$s - t = 6$

written another way,

$t = s - 6$

check by using

$s = 10$ and $t = 4$

DID YOU KNOW?

The opposite of squaring a number is <u>square rooting</u>.

For example: $6^2 = 36$

$\sqrt{36} = 6$

(or -6)

Test your knowledge 2

1 The first three diagrams in an expanding sequence are shown.

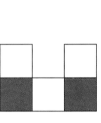 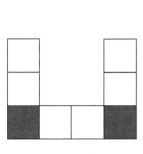 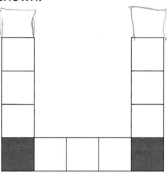

$n = 1$ $n = 2$ $n = 3$

a) Sketch the next diagram. **(1 mark)**

b) Complete the table. **(3 marks)**

n	1	2	3
White squares, w			
Black squares, s			
Total squares, t			

c) Write down and simplify an expression for the number of **(3 marks)**

   (i)   white squares
   (ii) black squares
   (iii) squares in total

2 For each table find an equation for the pattern, p, in terms of the position, n.

a)

n	1	2	3	4	5
p	8	11	14	17	20

(2 marks)

b)

n	1	2	3	4	5
p	2	6	10	14	18

(2 marks)

3 The area of a net of a cuboid that has two identical dimensions, s, and a third, t that is different, as shown in the diagram, can be found using the equation:

$A = 2s(s + 2t)$

Calculate A if

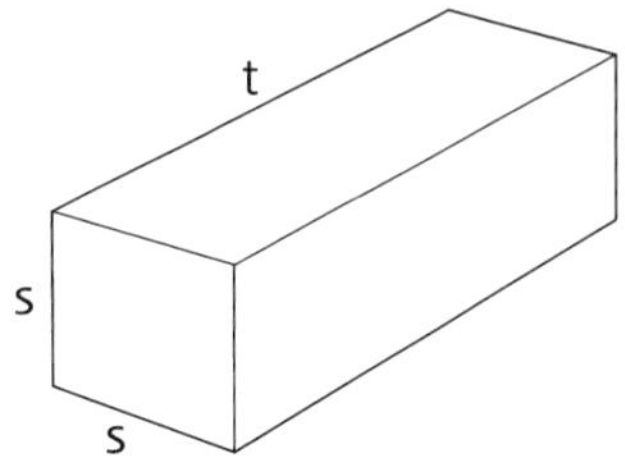

a) $s = 2$ and $t = 3$ **(2 marks)**

b) $s = 4$ and $t = 1$ **(2 marks)**

where s and t are in centimetres.

4 The equation for finding the area of an isosceles right-angled triangle is shown below.

$A = \dfrac{x^2}{2}$

Find the area of the triangle if

a) $x = 1$ **(2 marks)**

b) $x = 4$ **(2 marks)**

where x is in metres.

5 $p + q = 6$

Seven equations are shown. Some are equivalent to the equation above, others are not. Place a tick next to those that are equivalent, and a cross next to those that are not.

$p = 6 - q$
$p + 6 = q$
$p = q - 6$
$q = p - 6$
$q + p = 6$
$6 = q + p$
$q - p = 6$

(4 marks)

6 The following equations are all equivalent to each other:

$g = \dfrac{20}{h}$ $\qquad gh = 20 \qquad h = \dfrac{20}{g}$

For each question find the value stated.

a) $h = 2$, find g. **(1 mark)**

b) $g = 5$, find h. **(1 mark)**

c) $g = 0.1$, find h. **(2 marks)**

(Total 27 marks)

Lawn yawn

The grass on the village green needs replacing before next summer's croquet competition. Ralph has offered to find out the costs for replacing the lawn. He also needs to find out what length of fence is needed to go around the lawn.

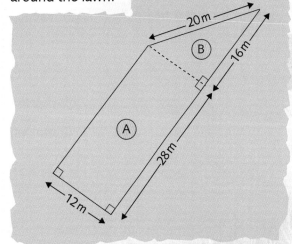

To find the area of the lawn, you need to know how to find the area of rectangles and <u>triangles</u>.

Area of rectangle A = base × height = $12 \times 28 = 336 \, \text{m}^2$
Area of triangle B = half base × height = $16 \times 12 \div 2 = 96 \, \text{m}^2$

Total lawn area = $336 + 96 = 432 \, \text{m}^2$

To find the perimeter just add up **all** the sides:

Perimeter = $20 + 16 + 28 + 12 + 28 =$ **104 m**

Clever Max knows a quicker way to do it since he realises that the lawn is a <u>trapezium</u>.

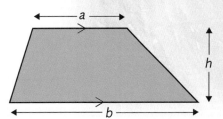

Area of trapezium = $(a + b) \times \dfrac{h}{2}$

h is the **perpendicular** height

$A = (28 + 44) \times \dfrac{12}{2} = 72 \times 12 \div 2 =$ **432 m²**

Perimeter puzzle

The shape shown has an area of 8 cm². All the squares are joined edge to edge.

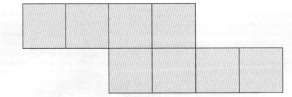

1 Find the perimeter of the shape.

   More squares are added to the shape, edge to edge.

2 What is the minimum (smallest) number of squares that need to be added to increase the perimeter to 20 cm²?

3 What is the maximum (largest) number of squares that can be added to increase the perimeter to 20 cm²?

• TOP TIPS •

• **Learn the area formulae for rectangles and triangles:**

h

b

• **Area of rectangle = $b \times h$**

h

b

• **Area of triangle = $\frac{b}{2} \times h$**

• **Don't get area and perimeter muddled up. They are different things.**

DID YOU KNOW?

Some people think that the area is always a larger number than the perimeter. In fact it just depends on the dimensions of the shape.

Look at these three rectangles all with area 18 cm².

18 cm

1 cm

Perimeter =

2(18) + 2(1) = 38 cm

6 cm

3 cm

Perimeter =

2(6) + 2(3) = 18 cm

4 cm

4.5 cm

Perimeter =

2(4) + 2(4.5) = 17 cm

Birthday boxes

Izzy's friend Kate is having a birthday meal on Saturday. Izzy has bought a present, which she has decided to wrap in a homemade card box, but she isn't sure how to cut out the card so that it folds up correctly.

The two-dimensional shape that folds up to make a solid shape is called a <u>net</u>.

There are several ways to make a net for a cube.

An easy one is:

But there are lots more. All of these nets fold up to make a cube, except one. Which one?

Ribbon riddle

A gift shop makes cuboid boxes for wrapping presents. The boxes look as though they have a ribbon around them. The ribbon needs to be drawn on the net so that it looks like this when folded up, with the ribbon going all the way around.

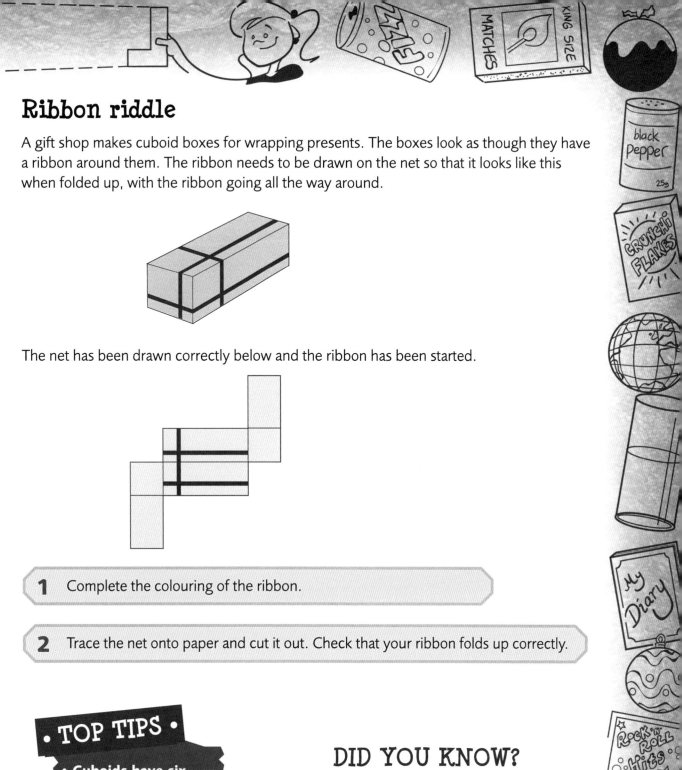

The net has been drawn correctly below and the ribbon has been started.

1 Complete the colouring of the ribbon.

2 Trace the net onto paper and cut it out. Check that your ribbon folds up correctly.

DID YOU KNOW?

These are the names of the different parts of a solid.

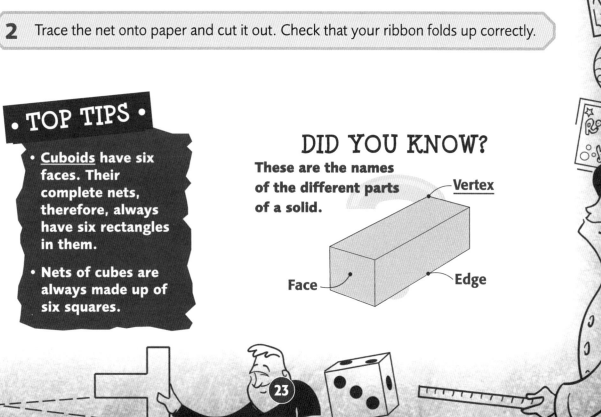

Vertex

Face

Edge

Kite flying

Ralph is reminiscing about how he used to make and fly kites when he was younger. He's trying to show Izzy some of his designs on graph paper but he keeps getting confused.

Ralph has put A at (5, 5) and D at (2, 3). Izzy has had to help out by finishing the <u>kite</u> shape in red.

Max has seen another way that Izzy could have finished the kite. He puts C at (2, 7) and B at (0, 5). Have a go at plotting the points.

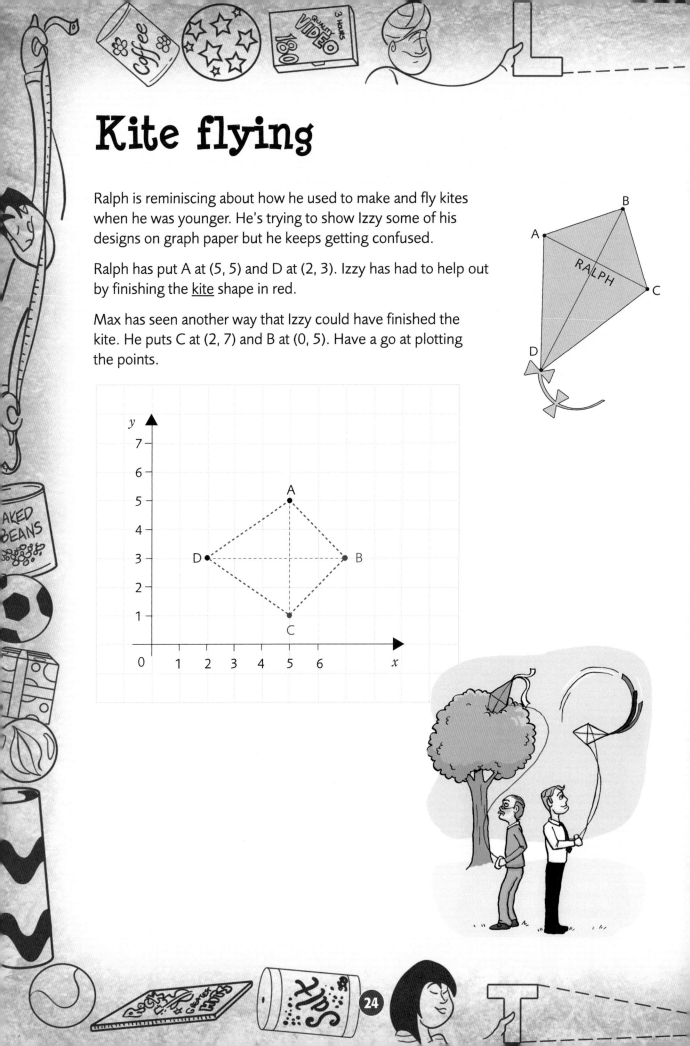

Coordinate corner

Three corners, A, B, and C, of a <u>quadrilateral</u> are shown.

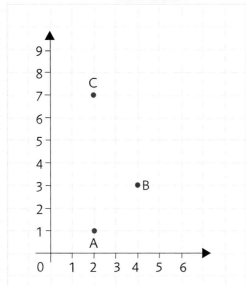

Write down the possible coordinates of the fourth corner if the shape is to be:

1 a kite

2 a <u>parallelogram</u>.

DID YOU KNOW?

The corners of shapes like rectangles, kites and so on should be labelled A, B, C, D around the perimeter in order.

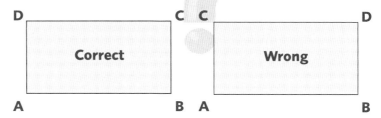

Test your knowledge 3

1 Find the area and perimeter of each shape.

a)

5 cm

3 cm

(2 marks)

b)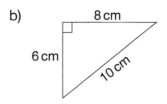

8 cm

6 cm

10 cm

(2 marks)

2 Find the dimensions of a rectangle that has the same value for both its area and its perimeter.

(2 marks)

3 The net below is folded up to form a cube. List all the points that join together at the vertices of the cube.

(3 marks)

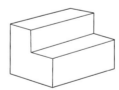

G   F

E

H   D

J   C

A   B

4 A solid is shown.

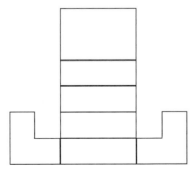

The net of the solid is being drawn. One face of the solid is missing from the net.

In how many different positions can the final face be included in the net if edges are joined to edges? Sketch each solution in the space provided.

(4 marks)

5 The graph shows two points A and B on a straight line.

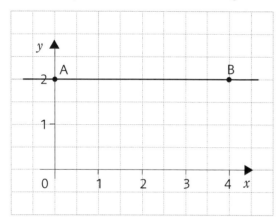

a) Write down the coordinates of the points A and B. **(2 marks)**

   A (,)   B (,)

b) Write down the coordinates of two other points on the line AB. **(2 marks)**

c) A triangle is made using A and B as vertices. The triangle is isosceles and right-angled so that AB is the longest side. What are the possible coordinates of the third vertex?

(2 marks)

6 Using a sketch if you wish, describe the shapes that have vertices with the following coordinates:

a) A (0, 4)   B (3, 0)   C (0, 0)   **(2 marks)**

b) A (3, 0)   B (5, 0)   C (4, 3)   **(2 marks)**

c) A (0, 3)   B(4, 3)   C (5, 0)   D (0, 0)   **(2 marks)**

(Total 25 marks)

Alphabet soup

Max is making soup for himself and Izzy to share when she gets home from school. For a change, and a bit of fun, he is adding pasta in the shape of letters to the soup. But what are the chances of picking a letter in Izzy's name?

Before adding the pasta, Max has counted all the letters.

A	B	C	D	E	F	G	H	I	J	K	L	M
15	0	1	2	20	1	2	2	10	1	2	6	6

N	O	P	Q	R	S	T	U	V	W	X	Y	Z
4	14	4	1	4	6	5	5	1	2	1	4	2

There are 120 letters in total.

Max is wondering about this question:

If Izzy takes out a letter without looking, what is the probability that it is one of the letters in her name?

Remember how probabilities work.

There are three different letters in her name: I, Z and Y.

In the soup there are 10 Is, 2 Zs and 4 Ys = 16.

Probability of picking an I, Z or Y $= \dfrac{16}{120}$

$$= \dfrac{8}{60}$$

$$= \dfrac{4}{30}$$

$$= \dfrac{2}{15}$$

Mint condition

At the end of each year, maths textbooks are collected in and their condition is assessed.

160 books were collected in from Year 8.

Condition	Number
As new	30
Very good	45
Good	60
Fair	x
Poor	10

1 What is the probability of a Year 7 pupil getting one of these books next year that is in at least good condition?

2 How many books are in 'fair' condition?

3 Imagine the teacher is handing all the books to you one after the other to pass out to the class. You can sneakily keep the first book you like the look of. You want a book that is in 'good' condition or better. How many books must the teacher give you before you're certain to have one you would be willing to keep?

• TOP TIPS •

- **Probability of event**
  = number of ways of getting what you want / total number of possible results

- You should always cancel down a fraction if you can. This is called getting the fraction into its 'simplest form'.

  e.g. $\frac{3}{12} = \frac{1}{4}$

- Never refer to a probability as, for example, '1 in 4'.

DID YOU KNOW?

Probabilities are often given as fractions such as $\frac{2}{5}$. And you sometimes see them written as decimals (0.4) or percentages (40%). They all mean the same thing.

Calculator brain

Izzy was in a rush this morning and left her calculator at home. Her teacher will not let her borrow one.

The first problem is 29 × 53. It's not too horrible-looking but how can she do it?

Izzy splits up the problem:

Adding the squares gives an answer of 1537.

It is important to be able to do calculations without a calculator like this. There are other ways though.

this line is (29 × 3)

this line is (29 × 50)

$$
\begin{array}{r}
29 \\
\times\ 53 \\
\hline
87 \\
1450 \\
\hline
1537
\end{array}
$$

You're the teacher

A student is trying to do the calculation 232 × 240 without a calculator.

He has written the following.

	200	30	2
200	4000	6000	400
40	240	1200	42

There are three mistakes in his working.

1 Find each mistake and circle it.

2 Correct each mistake.

3 Find the answer to 232 × 240 without using a calculator.

• TOP TIPS •

It's always a good idea to check your answer by doing an estimate. For the question 232 × 240 you might do 200 × 250 = 50000. You can use estimation like this whether or not you are using a calculator.

DID YOU KNOW?

Some questions are easily simplified. For example, with 5.5 × 6 you can double one if you halve the other.

$$5.5 \times 6 = 11 \times 3 = 33$$

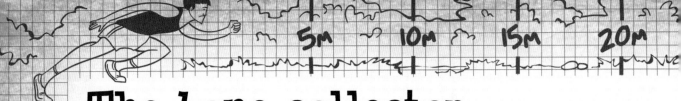

The bone collector

Spotless seems to have developed an amazing way of burying his bones. In different parts of the garden there are numbers of bones buried in larger and larger patterns. These are obvious from the earth mounds above them.

The patterns are like this:

1st pattern

2nd pattern

3rd pattern

4th pattern

When given patterns like this it is important to be able to recognise common ones and predict how many objects there will be in larger patterns.

This bone pattern is 'triangle numbers'. These are often seen as single dots or squares.

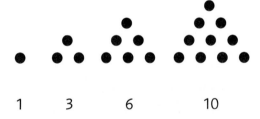

| 1 | 3 | 6 | 10 |

The number of extra dots in each pattern increases by one each time. The next pattern will have 15 dots in it.

Another common pattern is square numbers.

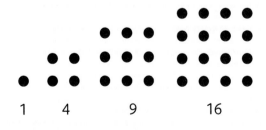

| 1 | 4 | 9 | 16 |

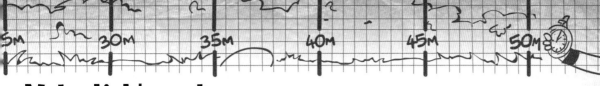

Make light work

A company makes floodlights for sports stadiums in different sizes. Larger sizes have more lamps in them.

Size 1   Size 2   Size 3   Size 4

1 By drawing a sketch, work out how many lamps there are in size 5 floodlights.

2 Without drawing a sketch of the pattern, work out how many lamps there are in size 10 floodlights.

3 The largest size floodlight available has 272 lamps in it. Find the size number for this floodlight.

• TOP TIPS •

When looking at sequences, work out the differences between numbers. There will be a pattern in them, even if they are changing.

DID YOU KNOW?

The Fibonacci sequence was discovered about 800 years ago by Leonardo Fibonacci. Each number is the two previous ones added up!

1, 1, 2, 3, 5, 8, 13, 21...

$x+2=4a+6$

$3y+2=z$

$y-1x=6z$

5M   30M   35M   40M   45M   50M

Test your knowledge 4

1 MISSISSIPPI

A letter is chosen at random from the word Mississippi. What is the probability that the letter is:

a) an M? **(1 mark)**

b) a consonant? **(2 marks)**

c) an A? **(1 mark)**

2 20 pupils in a class are asked what colour hair they have and what colour their eyes are. The results are shown in the table.

	Brown eyes	Blue eyes
Blonde hair	3	12
Brown hair	4	1

One pupil in the class had brown hair and blue eyes.

A pupil is chosen from the class at random. What is the probability that the pupil

a) has blonde hair and blue eyes? **(2 marks)**

b) has brown hair? **(2 marks)**

c) has brown eyes? **(2 marks)**

3 An expanding pattern is shown. How many circles are there in the 5th diagram?

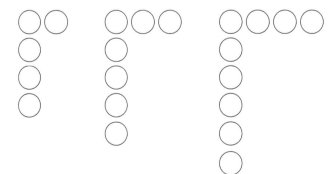

(2 marks)

4 Two rectangles are highlighted in this shape.

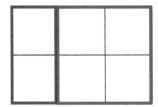

   a) How many squares are there in the shape?   **(2 marks)**

   b) How many rectangles are there in the shape?   **(2 marks)**

5 Calculate the following without using a calculator. Show your working.

   a) 465×12 **(2 marks)**

   b) 49×64 **(2 marks)**

6 Calculate the following without using a calculator. Show your working.

   a) 16×12.5 **(2 marks)**

   b) $9 \times 16\frac{1}{3}$ **(2 marks)**

                                                          (Total 24 marks)

Timing is everything

Max is cooking roast chicken for Sunday lunch. He's told everyone that it will be ready at one o'clock, so he will have to time the cooking carefully to get it right.

Unfortunately, every bird takes a different time to cook depending on its weight. This week it's a 7 lb bird, so when should he start cooking? Is there a general rule he can use?

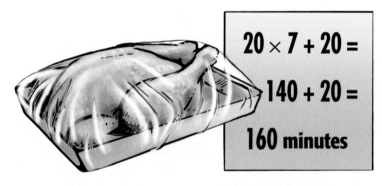

$20 \times 7 + 20 =$

$140 + 20 =$

160 minutes

A rough rule for chicken is 20 minutes for every pound in weight plus an extra 20 minutes.

So, for the 7 lb bird, he should cook it for 20 × 7 + 20 = 140 + 20 = 160 minutes. That's 2 hrs and 40 mins. Max should start cooking the chicken at 10:20am at the latest.

The rule for cooking chicken can be written as a mathematical rule. It will include letters for time, T (minutes), and weight, W (lbs).

$$T = 20W + 20$$

This sort of rule has an equals sign and is called an <u>equation</u>.

Number wall

The number in each block in this 'wall' is the total of the two numbers immediately below it.

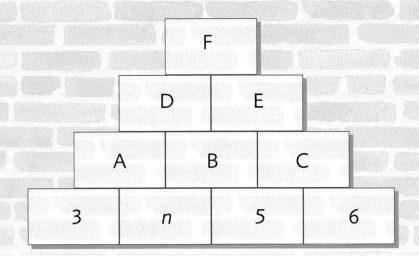

1 Write down an equation for each of the blocks in the top three layers. The first one has been done for you.

A = n + 3
B =
C =
D =
E =
F =

2 If the top block is 45, what's the missing number, n, in the bottom row?

TOP TIPS

You need to know how to 'simplify' in algebra.

Here are four examples of the simplications you need to be able to do:

- $n + n = 2n$
- $2a + a + 3 + 4 = 3a + 7$
- $4(m + 2) = 4m + 8$
- $y \times y = y^2$

DID YOU KNOW?

Triangle numbers go 1, 3, 6, 10, 15...

The bricks in the puzzle are in a triangle pattern, so the total number of bricks will always be in the triangle number sequence.

Paper aeroplanes

Archie, a boy in Izzy's maths class, has been caught making paper planes. The teacher has decided that, instead of a punishment, Archie should show the class how the paper can make different shapes when it's folded.

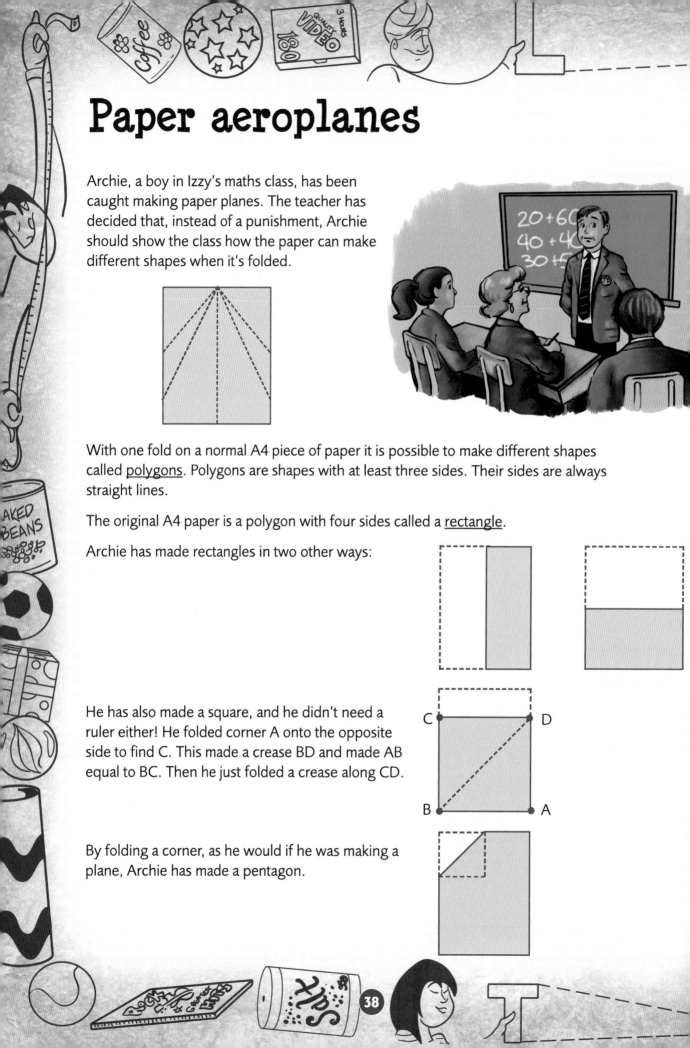

With one fold on a normal A4 piece of paper it is possible to make different shapes called <u>polygons</u>. Polygons are shapes with at least three sides. Their sides are always straight lines.

The original A4 paper is a polygon with four sides called a <u>rectangle</u>.

Archie has made rectangles in two other ways:

He has also made a square, and he didn't need a ruler either! He folded corner A onto the opposite side to find C. This made a crease BD and made AB equal to BC. Then he just folded a crease along CD.

By folding a corner, as he would if he was making a plane, Archie has made a pentagon.

Jigsaw pieces

You need some A4 size card or paper and some scissors. Cut the card into two equal halves with an angled cut as shown:

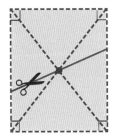

The cut must be straight and go through the centre of the page. The centre is where the two diagonals meet.

Your challenge is to join the two halves edge to edge to make new polygons. When you've made each one, draw a sketch so you don't forget how you did it. The first one has been done for you.

a) Parallelogram

b) Trapezium

c) Pentagon

d) Hexagon

e) Heptagon

f) Octagon

• TOP TIPS •

- **Trapezium – two sides parallel to each other and two that are not**

- **Pentagon – five sides**

- **Hexagon – six sides**

- **Heptagon – seven sides**

- **Octagon – eight sides**

- **A polygon is only regular if all its sides are the same length and all its interior angles the same size.**

DID YOU KNOW?

A circle can be thought of as a polygon with an infinite number of sides. The more sides a regular polygon has, the more it looks like a circle.

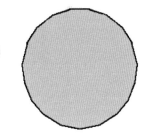

Recipe

Izzy has found an old cookery book that contains a recipe for steak and kidney with mushrooms. She wants to try the recipe but needs to convert the amounts into metric before going shopping.

Here is the recipe:

Steak and Kidney with Mushrooms
(12 Servings)
3 lb stewing steak
12 oz ox kidney
2 oz flour
2 large onions
10 oz mushrooms
$1\frac{1}{2}$ pints chicken stock

1 ounce (oz) ≈ 30 g
1 pound (lb) = 16 oz
1 pint ≈ $\frac{1}{2}$ litre (l)
1 gallon ≈ 8 pints

Izzy works out the amounts she needs in metric measures using the conversion table above.

3 lb steak = 3 × 16 oz = 48 oz = 48 × 30 g = 1440 g = 1.44 kg steak

12 oz kidney = 12 × 30 g = 360 g kidney

2 oz flour = 2 × 30 g = 60 g flour

10 oz mushrooms = 10 × 30 g = 300 g mushrooms

$1\frac{1}{2}$ pts stock = $1\frac{1}{2} \times \frac{1}{2}$ l = $\frac{3}{4}$ l = 750 ml stock

Can you convert them?

You will need to use the conversions on both these pages to do the following questions.

1 Find the correct conversions to the units shown.

   a) 2.45 m   = ... cm

   b) 750 ml   = ... l

   c) 40 inches   = ... ft

   d) 36 oz   = ... lb

2 Find approximate conversions to the units shown.

   a) 10 m   ≈ .... ft

   b) 100 km   ≈ .... miles

   c) 16 gallons   ≈ l

   d) 12 inches   ≈ .... cm

• TOP TIPS •

• **Learn these approximate conversions:**

1 metre ≈ 3 feet
1 kilogram ≈ 2.2 lb
1 inch (1") ≈ $2\frac{1}{2}$ cm
8 miles = 5 km

• **Other essential facts:**

10 mm = 1 cm   **100 cm = 1 m**
1000 g = 1 kg   **1 yard = 3 ft**
12 inches = 1 foot (ft)
1 l = 1000 ml

60 seconds in a minute and 60 minutes in an hour

DID YOU KNOW?

If you are converting from a smaller unit (e.g. mm) to a bigger one (e.g. m), you will end up with a smaller number, e.g. 2300 mm = 2.3 m

Test your knowledge 5

1 Two ways of measuring temperature are degrees Fahrenheit (°F) and degrees Celsius (°C). They are called temperature scales.

The diagram shows an approximate connection between Fahrenheit (F) and Celsius (C).

C	C	30
F		

For example, if C = 10, F = 10 + 10 + 30 = 50°F

a) Write down an equation connecting C and F. **(2 marks)**

b) If C = 16, find F. **(2 marks)**

c) If F = 130, find C. **(2 marks)**

2 Each brick in the wall is the total of the three bricks beneath it.

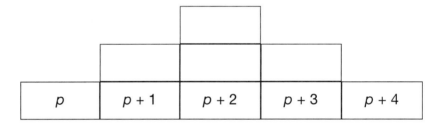

a) Complete the wall by filling in the empty bricks.
Simplify your answers. **(4 marks)**

b) Find the value of the top brick if $p = 2$. **(2 marks)**

c) If the top brick is 9 find p. **(2 marks)**

3 Fill in the missing measures.

a) 13.2 m = ... cm **(1 mark)**

b) 6700 mm = ... m **(1 mark)**

c) 25 miles ≈ .... km **(1 mark)**

d) 15 ft ≈ .... m **(1 mark)**

e) 562 g = ... kg **(1 mark)**

f) 1250 ml = ... l **(1 mark)**

4 A regular hexagon is cut into two identical (congruent) pieces. Each piece is half of the original hexagon.

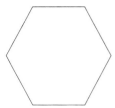

Draw sketches to show how this can be done so that each of the pieces separately are in the shape of a

a) Trapezium

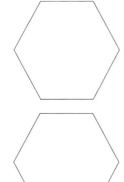

(2 marks)

b) Pentagon

(2 marks)

5 The right-angled triangle shown is to be cut into two pieces. This can be done in three different ways.

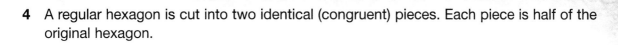

In three separate sketches, show how the triangle should be cut if the two resulting pieces are to be:

a) A right-angled triangle and a scalene triangle   **(2 marks)**

b) Two right-angled triangles   **(2 marks)**

c) An isosceles triangle and a second, different triangle.   **(2 marks)**

(Total 30 marks)

Catching the bus

Izzy travels almost everywhere by bus. She always keeps hold of all her tickets so she can ask her dad for the correct 'bus money' at the end the week.

Her dad has asked her to fill in a tally table and draw bar and pie charts to show the data.

Price (£)	Tally	Frequency
0.60	I	1
0.80	IIII	4
1.00	I	1
1.20	II	2

Note – a tally of 7 would look like this:

|||| ||

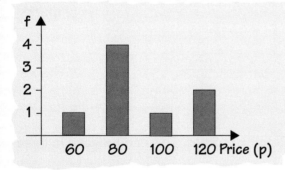

$360° ÷ 8 = 45°$ each ticket
1 ticket = $45°$
2 tickets = $90°$
4 tickets = $180°$

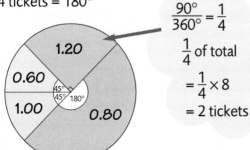

$$\frac{90°}{360°} = \frac{1}{4}$$

$\frac{1}{4}$ of total

$= \frac{1}{4} \times 8$

= 2 tickets

...days till we break up!

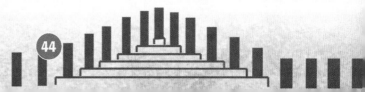

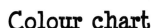

Colour chart

A class of 18 pupils has drawn a pie chart of their favourite colours. Work out how many pupils liked each colour.

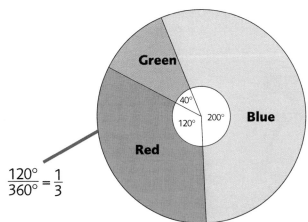

$$\frac{120°}{360°} = \frac{1}{3}$$

Complete the calculations.

Red	$\frac{1}{3}$	of	18	=	$\frac{1}{3}$	×	18	=	$\frac{18}{3}$	=	6

Blue		of	18	=		×	18	=	

Green		of	18	=		×	18	=	

• TOP TIPS •

- In a pie chart, the angle of each <u>sector</u> out of 360° is its fraction of the whole.

- In the pie chart on page 44, the 90° sector is $\frac{90}{360} = \frac{1}{4}$ of the total.

  1.20 angle is $\frac{1}{4}$ of all tickets. That is 8 ÷ 4 = 2 tickets. This is how many £1.20 tickets there were in the first place.

DID YOU KNOW?

Some ways of showing data are better than others. Pie charts are very good at giving you an idea of which category (sector) is the largest or smallest. They don't tell you how many things (or people) are in each one though. When you look at a bar chart you can tell how many things are in each category by reading the bar height

Cycleogically speaking

Ralph has invented a tricycle. It is an engineering marvel with no gears. The chain goes around two small wheels called cogs. The large cog goes round with the pedals. The small cog drives the wheels at the back.

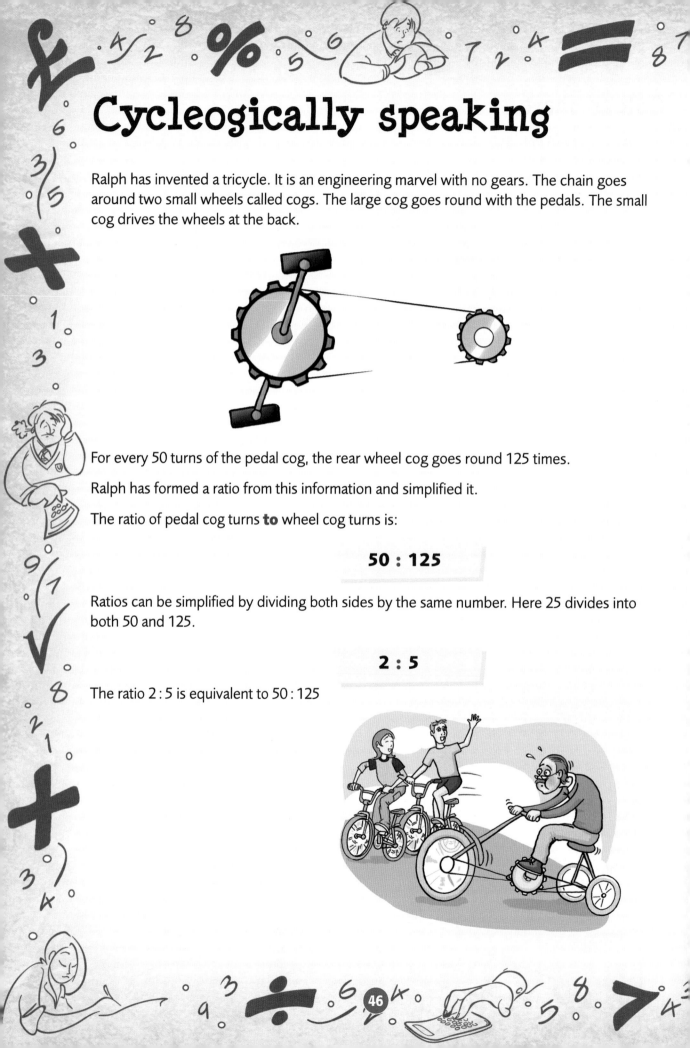

For every 50 turns of the pedal cog, the rear wheel cog goes round 125 times.

Ralph has formed a ratio from this information and simplified it.

The ratio of pedal cog turns **to** wheel cog turns is:

50 : 125

Ratios can be simplified by dividing both sides by the same number. Here 25 divides into both 50 and 125.

2 : 5

The ratio 2 : 5 is equivalent to 50 : 125

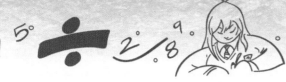

What's the ratio?

1 Complete the table by filling in the missing parts of each ratio. The ratios in each row are equivalent. The first row has been done for you.

1 : 2	4 : 8	21 : 42
1 : 5	3 :	: 55
12 : 1	24 :	: 5
3 : 2	9 :	: 14
4 : 7	20 :	: 49

2 £448 is to be shared between two people in the ratio of 5 : 3. How much should each person receive?

• TOP TIPS •

You need to read ratios carefully. The meaning will be stated in the question. For example, 'pedal cog turns to wheel cog turns' of 50 : 125 tells you exactly what the two numbers in the ratio relate to. A ratio of 125 : 50 would mean something completely different here.

DID YOU KNOW?

Ratios can involve three parts, e.g. 8 : 4 : 1. For example, if a lottery win of £130 was to be shared between three family members in this ratio, the money would be split up as £80, £40 and £10.

Afternoon feast

Izzy has spent the morning baking. She's made 12 biscuits and 18 cupcakes. She decides to invite some of her friends over to share them but is uncertain how many to ask. She wants everyone to have the same number of cakes and biscuits.

She could invite 2 friends so there would be 3 people altogether. 3 is a common <u>factor</u> of 12 and 18. Including herself, they would each get 4 biscuits and 6 cakes. But she'd like to invite more than two friends and still wants to share the food fairly.

So, that's one for you, one for you and one for me.

The largest number that divides into both 12 and 18 a whole number of times is 6. Since 6 is a factor common to both 12 and 18 and is the highest factor of both, it is called the <u>highest common factor</u>. This means that Izzy and 5 friends would get 2 biscuits and 3 cakes each.

To find the <u>lowest common multiple</u> of two numbers, write out the first few <u>multiples</u> of each number.

To find the lowest common multiple of 12 and 18:

12	24	**36**	48
18	**36**	54	72

The first number to appear in both lists is 36. This is the lowest common multiple of 12 and 18.

Fill the gaps

Fill in the blanks with the correct words or numbers.

multiples

4

1 The numbers 1, 2, 3, 4, 6, 8, 12 and 24 are the .... of 24.

72

2 The numbers 30, 60, 90, 120 and 150 are some of the .... of 30.

5

3 The factors of 30 are 1, 2, 3, ..., ..., ..., 15 and 30.

10

4 The first six multiples of 24 are 24, 48, ..., ..., ..., 144.

6

5 The highest common factor of 24 and 30 is ....

1

120

6 The lowest common multiple of 24 and 30 is ....

96

3

factors

7 The only square number that is a factor of 24 is ....

2

8 The factors of 30 that are prime numbers are ...., ...and ....

• TOP TIPS •

• Factors of a number can be paired. The factors of 18 are 1, 2, 3, 6, 9 and 18. These can be written as 1 × 18, 2 × 9, 3 × 6.

• Putting them in order starting with the smallest number on the left helps you organise your work.

DID YOU KNOW?

You can think of multiples as being the numbers in a times table. Think of the 6 times table:

6 × 1 = 6, 6 × 2 = 12, 6 × 3 = 18, 6 × 4 = 24...

The answers 6, 12, 18, 24... are the multiples of 6!

A prime number is a number that has exactly two factors. 3 is a prime number – its factors are 1 and 3. 1 is not a prime as it only has one factor.

Test your knowledge 6

1   Pupils in a year group were asked which was their favourite subject from Maths, English and Science. The results are shown in a bar chart.

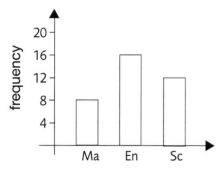

a) How many pupils preferred Science?   **(1 mark)**

b) How many more pupils preferred English to Maths?   **(2 marks)**

c) How many pupils were included in the survey?   **(2 marks)**

d) What fraction of the pupils surveyed preferred Maths?   **(2 marks)**

2   The newspapers bought by 120 teachers are included in a survey. There were just three different papers bought. The results are shown in a pie chart.

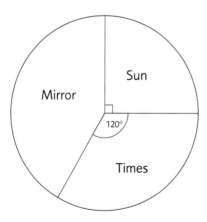

a) What fraction of the papers bought are *The Sun*?   **(1 mark)**

b) How many teachers bought *The Sun*?   **(1 mark)**

c) How many teachers bought *The Times*?   **(2 marks)**

3   Gemma has been carefully simplifying the ratio 36:48 but has smudged some of her
    work. Fill in the missing parts of her working.

    36 : 48

    18 :

        : 12

    3 :

                                                                    (3 marks)

4   The ratio of rainy days to dry days in Newcastle is estimated to be 2:3.
    Next month has 30 days in it. How many rainy days might be expected in
    Newcastle next month?   **(3 marks)**

5   a) Find the lowest common multiple of 6 and 8.   **(2 marks)**

    b) Find the highest common factor of 24 and 48.   **(2 marks)**

6   The number 6 has four factors.

    The number 12 has six factors.

    Find a number greater than 10 that has:

    a) a total of 8 factors   **(2 marks)**

    b) only two factors.   **(2 marks)**

                                                               (Total 25 marks)

Field research

The big news in the village is that some crop circles have been found in a field not far from Izzy's house. She has decided to look them up on the internet and has found some impressive patterns.

This is the first picture she finds.

The pattern has one <u>line of symmetry</u>, which is shown in red. If the page was folded along this line, both halves of the shape would fit together exactly. This line is sometimes called a <u>mirror line</u>.

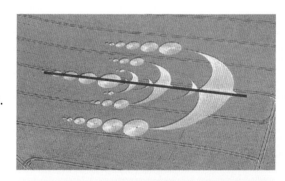

Some patterns have more than one line of symmetry.

This crop circle has a <u>hexagon</u> in it. Izzy has found 6 lines of symmetry. Three go through the hexagon's <u>vertices</u>. The other three go through the mid-points of the hexagon's sides. It can be easy to forget about or not notice these.

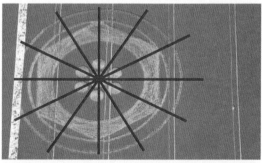

In this crop circle pattern there are no lines of symmetry.

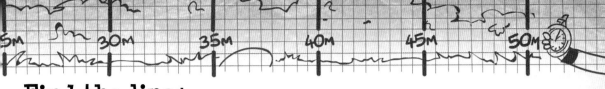
Find the lines

Draw **all** the lines of symmetry onto this regular octagon.
One has been done for you.

• TOP TIPS •

When reflecting a shape in a mirror line, all lines joining a point to its image go through the mirror line at 90° and come out the same distance on the other side.

DID YOU KNOW?

Some people believe crop patterns are made by visitors from space. Others think they are made by weather systems, such as tornadoes. Others believe they are all man-made.

$x+2=4a+6$

$3y+2=2$

$y-1x=6$

Reinventing the wheel

Ralph is trying out designs for the spokes of a new type of bicycle wheel.

He has cut a right-angled triangle out of card and is using it to trace an outline:

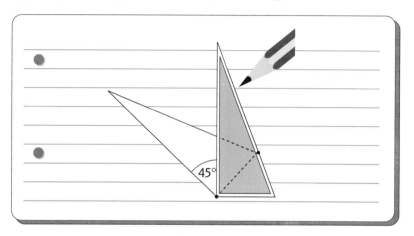

After tracing around the card, he then rotates it 45° about the centre of the wheel. When he's done this several times he has an outline of the wheel spokes.

The spokes look the same in eight positions. This means the shape has <u>rotational</u> <u>symmetry</u> of 'order 8'.

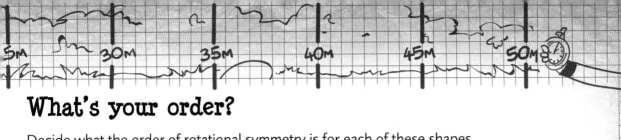
What's your order?

Decide what the order of rotational symmetry is for each of these shapes.

a)

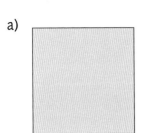

c)

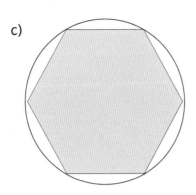

b)

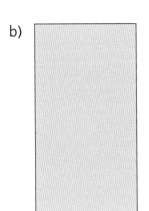

d)

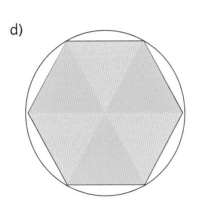

DID YOU KNOW?

Regular polygons (e.g. pentagon) always have rotational symmetry.

Irregular polygons may have some rotational symmetry, or none.

• TOP TIPS •

As a shape rotates, the number of positions where it looks the same is called the order of rotational symmetry. This number includes the starting position.

$x+z=4a+$

$3y+2=$

$y-1x=6$

Fly the flag

Max is enjoying an afternoon watching international cricket on the TV. Guyana are playing Australia. He has been distracted from the somewhat dull game by Guyanese flags being waved in the crowd.

He starts to think about how he might draw it. It is made up of a variety of triangles.

The red triangle is <u>isosceles</u>. Its base angles are the same. On this diagram they are the two angles on the left.

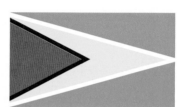

The angles on a line add up to 180°.

The angles in a triangle add up to 180°.

These facts are useful for solving problems like this one:

Find y.

It's an isosceles triangle because of the marks on two of the sides. The base is the side on the right. The third angle will be the same as y.

Since the three angles total 180°, the two angles not given must add up to $180° - 30° = 150°$.

These two angles are equal, so $y = 150 \div 2 = 75°$.

Another useful angle rule is shown here. When two lines cross, the opposite angles are the same. They are said to be **vertically opposite**.

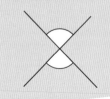

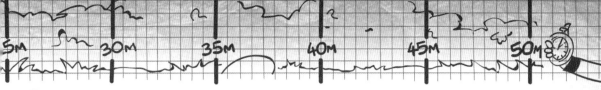

Fishy angles

A design for a fish logo to go on a T-shirt is made using a semi-circle and three straight lines. One angle is 50°, as shown. Find the angles *f* and *g*.

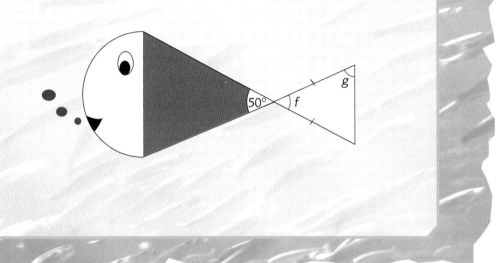

• TOP TIPS •

- The 'base' side of an isosceles triangle isn't equal to the other two sides in length. The two equal sides each have a mark on them.

- The base side isn't always at the bottom of the diagram.

DID YOU KNOW?

A triangle with all three sides equal in length is called an equilateral triangle. Since the three angles are the same and total 180°, each one is 180 ÷ 3 = 60°.

Test your knowledge 7

1 The angles in a triangle are *a*, *b* and *c* degrees. Complete the table.   **(5 marks)**

a	b	c
60°	20°	
40°		40°
35°	25°	
45°	90°	
2°		6°

2 Find angles *a* and *b*.   **(4 marks)**

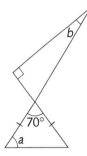

3 Two of the four sides of a quadrilateral have been drawn. They are each 3 cm long and make an angle of 90° to each other.

   (2 marks)

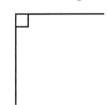

a) Sketch on the diagram the other two sides of the quadrilateral if it is to have rotational symmetry of order 4.

   Two 3 cm lines of a different quadrilateral are shown.   **(2 marks)**

b) Sketch on the diagram the other two sides of the quadrilateral if it is to have rotational symmetry

   (i) of order 2   **(2 marks)**

   (ii) of order 1   **(2 marks)**

4 A regular pentagon is shown. **(3 marks)**

Mark on all lines of symmetry on the diagram.

5 A magnetic compass has a needle that points to North. When the compass is moved, the needle rotates from a starting position of North. Here is an example:

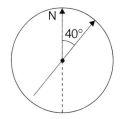

40° clockwise

For the other two compasses, draw on the position of the needle after the rotation described.

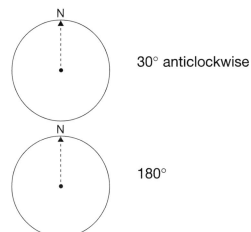

30° anticlockwise

180°

(3 marks)

6 A dotted mirror line is shown in each diagram. Complete the diagrams.

a) **(2 marks)**

b) **(2 marks)**

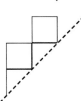

(Total 27 marks)

He loves me

Izzy and her friend Chloe both fancy the same boy in their class. In their lovestruck state, they've been picking daisies in the park. Chloe has challenged Izzy – whoever has more petals on their daisies on <u>average</u> can ask the boy out. They've each picked 10 daisies from different parts of the park, and have made a table of the number of petals.

He loves me.   He loves you NOT!

I	33	28	25	38	30	32	31	34	32	29
C	22	25	28	30	24	28	24	25	26	28

Key
Izzy = I
Chloe = C

Finding averages can be confusing. There are three different ones to learn: mean, median and mode.

- **Mode** – The most common number.

  Izzy = 32   Chloe = 28

- **Median** – The middle number, but they must be put in order first.

  Izzy = 25 28 29 30 31 32 32 33 34 38
  Chloe = 22 24 24 25 25 26 28 28 28 30

  As there is no middle number, it is half way between the 5th and 6th numbers.

  Izzy = 31.5   Chloe = 25.5

- **Mean** – Total ÷ how many numbers

  Izzy = 312 ÷ 10 = 31.2   Chloe = 260 ÷ 10 = 26

- **Range** is another method used for looking at data. It isn't an average but gives an idea of the spread of the data.

  Range = largest number – smallest number
  Izzy = 38 – 25 = 13   Chloe = 30 – 22 = 8

Alien averages

Annie and Brett have each played five rounds of 'Alien Shootout' on an arcade game.

Brett says that he was the only one to get a top score of 10 so he must be the best.

Annie's scores	9	5	9	7	5
Brett's scores	5	10	5	5	9

Calculate each of the following for their scores:

a)   mean

b)   mode

c)   median

d)   range

Do you agree with Brett?

DID YOU KNOW?

When someone talks about an average, for example in a newspaper, they are probably talking about the 'mean' rather than the mode or median.

Let sleeping dogs lie

Max has just come in with a heavy bag of shopping and almost tripped over Spotless, who is asleep in the doorway – again! Max has had enough of Spotless and his easy life and has decided to monitor what the dog does all day. He wants to work out what fraction of the day Spotless sleeps.

For 8 hours Max tries to record what Spotless is doing.

Here are his results:

3 hours sleeping and 1 hour walkies.

Spotless also spends $\frac{1}{4}$ of his time playing.

It's not too difficult to make sense of this information.

$\frac{1}{4}$ of the time playing is $\frac{1}{4}$ of 8 hours

$= \frac{1}{4} \times 8 = 8 \div 4 = 2$ hours

Using fractions throughout:

Sleeping $= \frac{3}{8}$

Walkies $= \frac{1}{8}$

Playing = 2 hours out of eight $= \frac{2}{8}$

Altogether this adds up to:

$\frac{3}{8} + \frac{1}{8} + \frac{2}{8} = \frac{6}{8}$

Cancelling down $\frac{6}{8} = \frac{3}{4}$.

This leaves $\frac{1}{4}$ of the time unaccounted for.

Fraction fill

Complete the table by filling in the empty cells.

$\frac{1}{2}$	of	24	=	
$\frac{1}{3}$	of	36	=	
$\frac{1}{4}$	of		=	5
$\frac{1}{6}$	of		=	12
	of	80	=	10
	of	132	=	11

• TOP TIPS •

Finding a fraction of a whole number is simply a matter of multiplying and then cancelling.

e.g. $\frac{3}{8} \times 32 = \frac{3 \times 32}{8}$

$= \frac{96}{8} = 96 \div 8 = 12$

DID YOU KNOW?

The top number in a fraction is called the **numerator**.

The bottom number in a fraction is called the **denominator**.

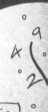

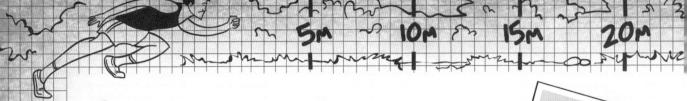

Sonar searches

Ralph has been telling Izzy about his time in the Navy as a sonar operator. Sonar is like radar but works underwater.

He remembers plotting the tracks of submarines that were trying to stay hidden underwater. He draws Izzy a sketch:

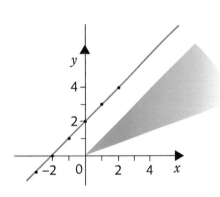

The dots form a line like some that are seen in maths. There are equations to describe such lines. In this graph the x coordinate is always 2 more than the y coordinate. So, the equation of the red line can be written as $y = x + 2$.

The table of coordinates for the line looks like this:

x	-2	-1	0	1	2	3
y	0	1	2	3	4	5

Here are some other lines that are seen frequently:

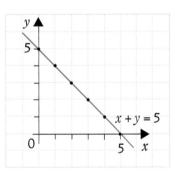

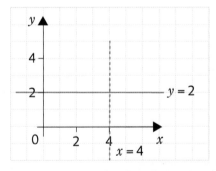

In this graph the points on the line include (2, 3), (4, 1) and (5, 0). The x and y coordinates in each case add up to 5. So the equation is $x + y = 5$.

In this graph the two lines are straight and either horizontal or vertical. Along the horizontal line the y coordinate is always 2, e.g. (0, 2) and (5, 2). The equation of this line is $y = 2$. On the vertical line there are points such as (4, 1) and (4, 3). Here the x coordinate is always 4. The equation of this line is therefore $x = 4$.

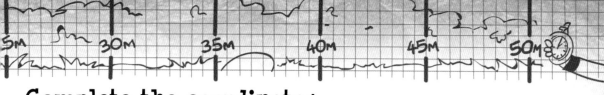

Complete the coordinates

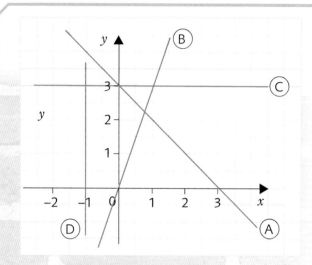

• TOP TIPS •

If you are asked to find the equation of a line, you should check that it works for more than just one pair of coordinates in the line. The equation must work for all pairs of coordinates on the line.

For each line complete the table of coordinates. Some have been done for you.

Line A

x	0	1	2	3	4
y	3				−1

Line B

x	0	1	2	3	4
y	0		6		

Line C

x	0	1	2	3
y	3		3	

Line D

x		−1		
y	0	1	2	3

DID YOU KNOW?

An equation of a line such as $x + y = 5$ can also be written as $y = -x + 5$. Equations are often written with y on its own on the left-hand side so that several different equations can be compared.

$x + 2 = 4a + 6$

$3y + 2 = z$

$y - 1x = 6z$

Test your knowledge 8

1 Four numbers are picked out of a hat without looking.

   2 6 4 0

   A fifth number is about to be taken out. What must this fifth number be if the set of five numbers is to have:

   a) a median of 3? **(2 marks)**

   b) a mode of 2? **(1 mark)**

   c) a mean of 4? **(2 marks)**

2 A manager has been monitoring attendance at work of his employees over the last two weeks.

   Here are the results:

Week 1	13	14	12	18	16
Week 2	13	12	13	11	?

   Find:

   a) The range of the data for Week 1.

   (2 marks)

   b) What are the possible attendances on the last day of Week 2 if the range for Week 2 is to be the same as Week 1? **(2 marks)**

3 Calculate the following without using a calculator.

   a) $\frac{1}{5} + \frac{3}{10}$ **(2 marks)**

   b) $\frac{3}{4} - \frac{3}{8}$ **(2 marks)**

   Give your answers as fractions in their simplest form.

4 A particular type of window glass allows only half the light on one side through. Three panes of glass are used in a triple glazed security window.

What fraction of the outside light passes through the window? **(2 marks)**

5 Four different lines are shown on the axes. **(2 marks)**

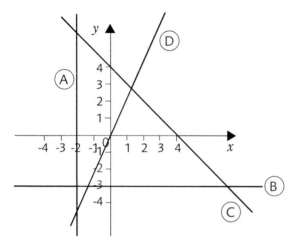

Write down the equation of each line.

(A) .... **(2 marks)**

(B) .... **(2 marks)**

(C) .... **(2 marks)**

(D) .... **(2 marks)**

6 Draw x and y axes each from 0 to 5.

a) On your axes sketch the lines $x = 1$ and $y = 3$. **(2 marks)**

b) Write down the point of intersection of the two lines. **(2 marks)**

(Total 27 marks)

Pocket money plea

Izzy has just asked her dad, Ralph, for more pocket money. Ralph is not amused, and tells her she should be grateful for what she gets. When he was young, his parents used to give him five times his age, in pence, as a weekly allowance.

Ralph's weekly allowance can be shown in a table. It can be used to spot patterns.

Age, a	6	7	8	9	10	...	12	....	16
Pence, P	30	35	40	45	50		60		80

The amounts from one year to the next go up by 5. This is a big clue as to what is happening. The jump of 5 shows what to multiply the age by to get the pocket money.

Pence, $P = 5 \times$ age, a

So $P = 5a$

This one is a bit more difficult.

p	1	2	3	4	5
q	4	7	10	13	16

The gap from one q to the next is 3. So q has something to do with three times p.

If you take any value of p in the table, say 4, and work out $3p$, you can work out what else is happening. When $p = 4$, $3p = 12$. But when $p = 4$ $q = 13$. So you need to add 1 to the 12. Therefore **$q = 3p + 1$**.

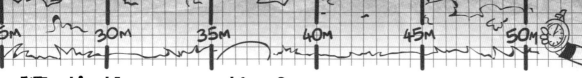

What's the connection?

For each table of values find the connection between *n* and the pattern.

1

n	1	2	3	4	5
a	5	9	13	17	21

2

n	1	2	3	4	5
b	3	7	11	15	19

3

n	1	2	3	4	5
c	2	7	12	17	22

4

n	1	2	3	4	5
d	5	6	7	8	9

• TOP TIPS •

It can sometimes be useful to work out the number that comes before the first number in the pattern. For the pattern 4, 7, 10, 13 etc. above, the number before the first term of 4 would be 1 (the gap is 3, remember). Notice we added on 1 to 3p to get the equation 3p + 1.

DID YOU KNOW?

The opposite point on the earth to where you are is called the 'antipode'. You can find the antipode by imagining a straight line that goes from where you are, through the centre of the earth, and out at the other side of the world. A trip to Australia is sometimes called an antipodean holiday because Australia is the antipode of Europe.

Time machine

Ralph has always dreamt of building a time machine that could transport him back to any date in history.

In his imaginary machine he would enter his age (53) into a computer and it would take this off the current year (2005) and divide that by 16. The resulting number would be the year he would be taken back to.

He has drawn a number machine to show what the computer would do:

| 2005 | ○○○○○▷ | − 53 | ○○○○○▷ | ÷ 16 | ○○○○○▷ | 122 |

It would take him back to 122, when Hadrian's Wall was built.

Assuming the number machine always does the same things (−53, ÷ 16), in what year would it be possible to travel back to the battle of Hastings in 1066?

| ? | ○○○○○▷ | − 53 | ○○○○○▷ | ÷ 16 | ○○○○○▷ | 1066 |

This can be done by guesswork, but it's a lot easier to reverse the computer's programme.

| ? | ○○○○○▷ | + 53 | ○○○○○▷ | × 16 | ○○○○○▷ | 1066 |

? = 1066 × 16 + 53 = **17 109**

Only 15 104 years to wait!

> I think I may have to adapt my calculations...

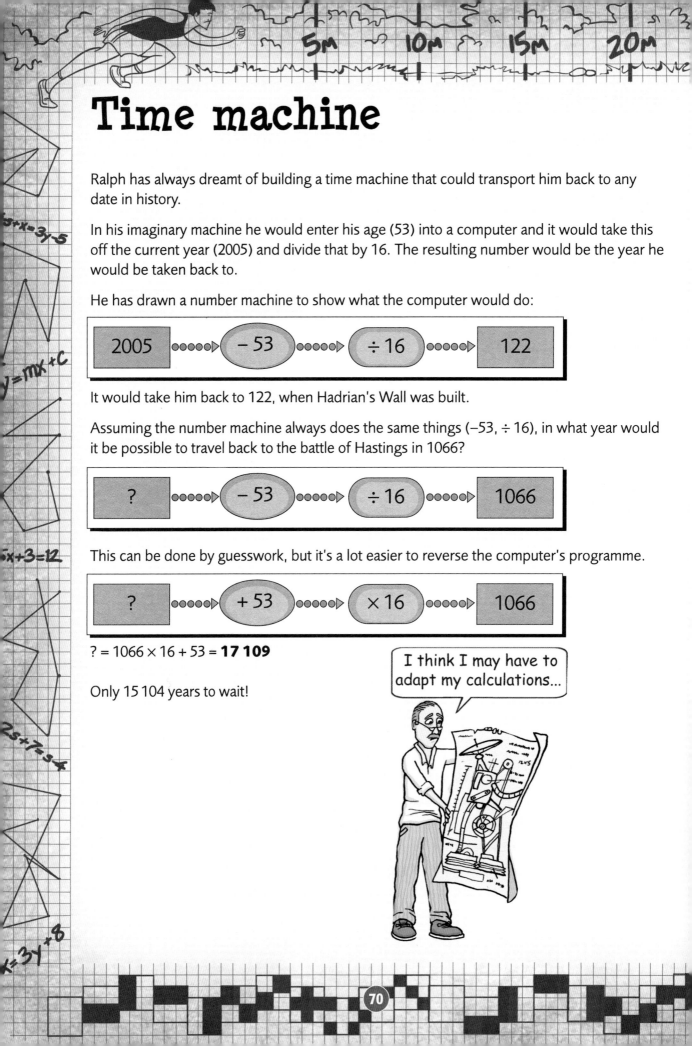

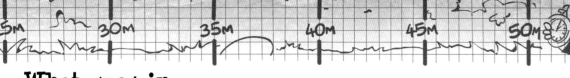

What goes in...

Here is a number machine:

1   Complete the table by filling in the missing inputs and outputs.

Input	Output
2	
5	
–2	
0	
	7
	16
	–14

DID YOU KNOW?

Number machines are the basis of computer programs. They are also a good starting point if you want to design an equation for use in a spreadsheet, such as Excel. Spreadsheets and programs do lots of calculations for you very quickly.

2   What number when put into the machine comes out the same?

- **Number machines are simple but the order of the boxes is very important. Usually, arrows show the direction and order in which to do things.**

- **Sometimes number machines can be simplified.**

| Input | → | + 5 | → | – 2 | → | Output |

| Input | → | + 3 | → | Output |

Here, the second machine does the same but with only one operation.

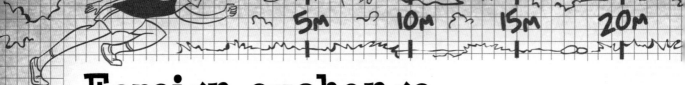
Foreign exchange

Ralph has bought a cheap second-hand mobile home and has asked Max to plan a camping holiday for all the family to Belgium.

Max doesn't want to drive more than 80 miles per day and he knows that distances on the continent are measured in kilometres. So how far will this be on Belgian road signs?

A good way to convert between two different measures is to use a simple graph.

5 miles = 8 kilometres   (Try to remember this…)

So 50 miles = 80 kilometres.

This is easily plotted at point A.

80 miles can be changed into km
using the red lines.
80 miles = 128 km.

Likewise 50 km = 31 miles (approximately)
using the green lines

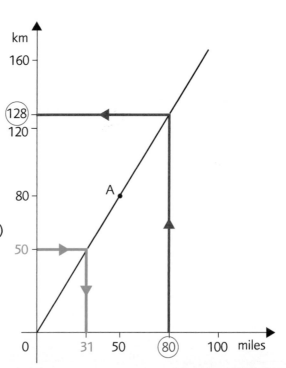

Currency converter

The exchange rate between English pounds and Australian dollars is £1 = $2.50.

1) How many Australian dollars is £100 worth?

2) Complete a conversion graph for this exchange rate
   and use it to find the value of $375 in £s.

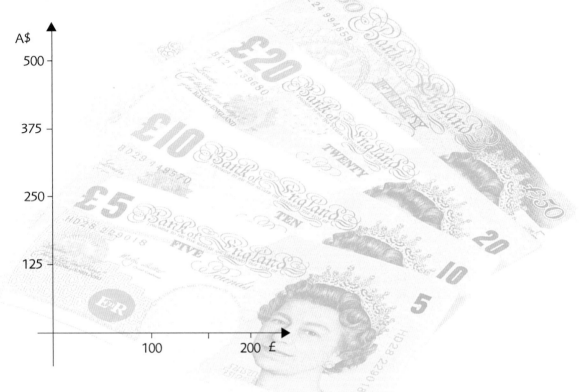

DID YOU KNOW?

Exchange rates change all the time.
There are often two rates for each
currency (e.g. £/$). One is the rate a
bank will sell to you, and the other
the rate at which they'll buy
currency back from you. The
difference is the bank's profit.

$x+z=4a+6$

$3y+2=2$

$y-1x=6$

Test your knowledge 9

1 A number machine is shown. **(5 marks)**

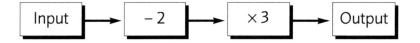

Complete the table of inputs and outputs.

Input	Output
4	
2	
1	
−2	
	−6

2 A number machine has two operations boxes. When a number is put into the machine its value after the first operation is '*v*'. **(2 marks)**

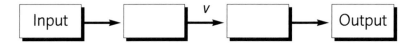

The following inputs lead to the outputs shown.

INPUT	v	OUTPUT
2	8	7
1	4	3
0	0	−1

Use this table of information to work out the operations in the machine.

3 Areas of land can be measured in acres and hectares. 1 hectare is $10\,000\,\text{m}^2$, or about 2.5 acres.

The conversion graph below is designed to convert between acres and hectares.

Use the conversion graph to change:

a) 60 hectares into acres **(1 mark)**

b) 50 acres into hectares **(1 mark)**

c) 24 hectares into acres **(1 mark)**

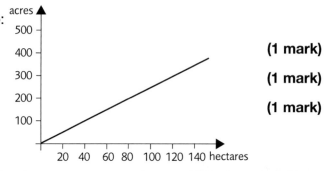

4 A conversion graph is to be drawn on the axes provided. 10 gallons is equal to approximately 45 litres.

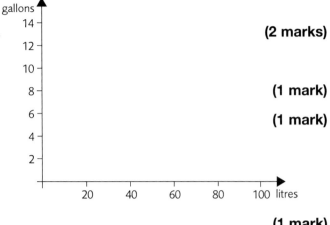

a) Complete the conversion graph. **(2 marks)**

b) Use your graph to find:

   (i) 14 gallons in litres **(1 mark)**

   (ii) 40 litres in gallons **(1 mark)**

   (iii) 200 litres in gallons. **(1 mark)**

5 A pattern begins as shown in the table.

p	1	2	3	4	5	......	12
t	4	9	14	?	?		?

a) What is the difference between one number and the next in the pattern? **(1 mark)**

b) Find the three missing numbers indicated in the table. **(3 marks)**

c) Write down an equation connecting p and t. **(2 marks)**

6 Four tables are given with different sequences. Expressions are given that each match with one of the tables.

Use arrows to link the each table to the correct equation.

a)

n	1	2	3	4
x	1	3	5	7

$2n + 1$ **(1 mark)**

b)

n	1	2	3	4
y	3	5	7	9

$3n - 1$ **(1 mark)**

c)

n	1	2	3	4
z	2	5	8	11

$3n + 1$ **(1 mark)**

d)

n	1	2	3	4
w	4	7	10	13

$2n - 1$ **(1 mark)**

(Total 25 marks)

Glossary

Average There are three different averages.
Mean = total of the numbers ÷ number of numbers
Mode = most frequently occurring number. There may be more than one mode.
Median = the middle number when all numbers are placed in size order.

Cuboid A solid with six faces.

Diagonal The line joining two vertices of a polygon.

Double Multiply a number by 2.

Equation An equation relates two expressions that are equivalent. An equation with one variable (letter) can be solved.

Equivalent Expressions are equivalent when they have the same meaning. One is usually a simpler way of writing the other.

Factor A number that divides into another number a whole number of times, e.g. 4 is a factor of 12.

Highest common factor The largest number that is a factor of two or more numbers in a question.

Isosceles An isosceles shape has two sides of equal length.

Kite A quadrilateral with two pairs of adjacent sides of equal length.

Line of symmetry The line that divides a shape into two identical halves.

Lowest common multiple The lowest common multiple of two or more numbers is the smallest number that they all go into a whole number of times without a remainder.

Mirror line This is the line of reflection used when generating a shape that has symmetry.

Multiples A multiple of a number is the number obtained by multiplying it by a whole number.

Net The 2-D shape that can be folded up to make a 3-D solid.

Parallelogram A quadrilateral with two pairs of sides opposite to each other that are parallel and equal in length.

Perimeter The distance around the outside of a shape.

Polygon A polygon is a two-dimensional shape with straight sides enclosing an area.

Polygons include triangles (3 sides), squares (4 sides), pentagons (5 sides), hexagons (6 sides), heptagons (7 sides), octagons (8 sides), nonagons (9 sides) and decagons (10 sides).

Positive Numbers greater than zero, e.g. 5.2, 9.

Quadrilateral Any four-sided polygon.

Rectangle A quadrilateral with two pairs of sides parallel and of equal length. All interior angles are 90°.

Rotational symmetry A shape has rotational symmetry when it can be rotated into a new position and still appear the same as it did in its original position.

Sector The area between two radii of a circle and part of the circumference.

NB The radius is the straight line or distance from the centre of a circle to a point on its circumference.

Square A polygon with four sides of equal length and four interior angles of 90°.

To square a number means to multiply it by itself. 3 squared = 3^2 = 9

Square root To square root a number means finding the number that, if squared, gives you the number you have to start with. The square root of 16 = $\sqrt{16}$ = 4 (or −4). NB $4^2 = (−4)^2 = 16$

Term A sequence or equation is made up from terms. Each term is one of the numbers in the sequence.

Trapezium A quadrilateral with one pair of parallel sides. The other pair of sides are not parallel.

Triangle A three-sided polygon.

Vertex (Vertices) The vertices of a shape or solid are its corners.

Answers

Magic squares p5

1) 2   2) 2   3) 5   4) 3

Magic Square: Middle row total = 5 + 1 − 3 = 3.
So all rows/columns/diagonals total 3.
Missing top row: 3, 2. Missing bottom row: 0, −1.

What's the letter p7

1) 4   2) 10   3) 1   4) 24   5) −1   6) 5

Making the square p9

D = 0.125   P = 80%

Expanding sequences p13

1) Purple 1, Orange 16, Red 40, White 24
2) Pink = 2, 3, 4, 5. Yellow = 2, 2, 2, 2. $p = N + 1$ $y = 2$

How many cards? p15

a) 24   b) $c = 2 \times 12 \times 8 = 192$

Equation match p17

A 3 B 2 C 2 D 1 E 3

Perimeter puzzle p21

1) 16 cm

2) 2, e.g.   3) 6, e.g.

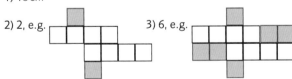

Ribbon riddle p23

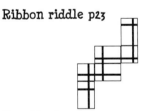

Coordinate corner p25

1 (0, 3)   2 (0, 5) or (4, 9)

Mint condition p29

1) $\frac{135}{160} = \frac{27}{32}$ 2) 15   3) 26

You're the teacher p31

1) 4000, 240, 42   2) 40000, 8000, 80
3) 40000 + 6000 + 400 + 8000 + 1200 + 80 = 55 680

Make light work p33

1) $5 \times 6 = 30$ lamps   2) $10 \times 11 = 121$ lamps
3) A good starting point is to notice that if 'n' is the size then n^2 is close to the number of lamps. The square root of 272 is 16.49... so it is size 16. Try $16 \times 17 = 272$!

Number wall p37

1) $B = n + 5$ $C = 11$ $D = 2n + 8$ $E = n + 16$ $F = 3n + 24$
2) $3n + 24 = 45$ $3n = 21$ $n = 7$

Jigsaw pieces p39

b)   d)

c)   or

e)   f)

Can you convert them? p 41

1) a) 100 cm = 1 m. 2.45 m = 2.45 × 100 cm = 245 cm
    b) 750 ml = $\frac{750}{1000}$ = 0.75 l
    c) 12 inches = 1 ft. 36 inches = 3 ft. 40 inches = 3 ft 4 ins (or $3\frac{1}{3}$ ft)
    d) 16 oz = 1 lb. 32 oz = 2 lb. 36 oz = 2 lb 4 oz
2) a) 1 m ≈ 3 ft. 10 m = 3 × 10 = 30 ft
    b) 8 km ≈ 5 miles. 100 km ≈ 100 × 5 ÷ 8 = 62.5 miles
    c) 1 gall ≈ 4.5 litres. 16 gall ≈ 16 × 4.5 = 72 l
    d) 1 ins ≈ 2.5 cm. 12 ins ≈ 12 × 2.5 = 30 cm

Colour chart p45

$\frac{200}{360} = \frac{5}{9}$ of 18 = $\frac{5}{9} \times 18$ = 10

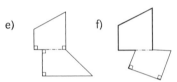
$\frac{40}{360} = \frac{1}{9}$ of 18 = $\frac{18}{2}$ = 2

What's the ratio? p47

1) 3:15   11:55
    24:2   60:5
    9:6   21:14
    20:35   28:49
2) 5:3 = 8 parts in total. £448 ÷ 8 = £56. 5 × 56 = £289. 3 × 56 = £168

Fill the gaps p49

1) factors   2) multiples   3) 5, 6, 10   4) 72, 96, 120
5) 6   6) 120   7) 4   8) 2, 3, 5

Find the lines p53

What's your order? p55

a) 4   b) 2   c) 6   d) 3

Fishy angles p57

f is vertically opposite the 50°. $f = 50°$
$180° - 50° = 130°$. $130° \div 2 = 65°$

Alien averages p61

a)   Annie = $35 \div 7 = 7$ Brett = $34 \div 5 = 6.8$
b)   Annie = 5   Brett = 5
c)   Annie = 7   Brett = 5
d)   Annie = $9 - 5 = 4$ Brett = $10 - 5 = 5$
    Annie's averages are better, though the modes are the
    same. Her marks are a little closer together as her range
    is a little less. So, you could say that overall Annie is a
    better and more consistent player.

Fraction fill p63

12   12   20   72 $\frac{1}{8}$ $\frac{1}{12}$

Complete the coordinates p65

A 2, 1, 0   B 3, 9, 12   C 3, 3   D –1, –1, –1

What's the connection? p69

1) $a = 4n + 1$ 2) $b = 4n - 1$ 3) $c = 5n - 3$
4) $d = n + 4$ (or $1n + 4$)

What goes in... p71

1)   outputs: 4, 17, –8, –2   inputs: 3, 6, –4
2)   If x = input and output, then $3x - 2 = x$, so $3x - x = +2$,
    and $2x = 2$, so $x = 1$

Currency converter p73

1   $250
2

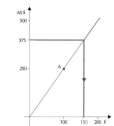

Test your knowledge 1

1   a)   –4   –3   2   5   7
b)   (i) 3   (ii) 3   (iii) 1   (iv) –2
2   a) $4 \times 4 = 16$ b) $11^2 = 121$
    c) $3 \times 3 = 9$ d) $5 \times -2 = -10$
3   a) $12 \div 4 = 3$ b) ± 5
    c) $(16 + 2) \div 3 = 6$ d) $(12 \div 2) - 2 = 4$
4   a)   3%   13%   30%   31%   33%
    b)   0.02   0.03   0.123   0.23   0.32

---

c) $\frac{1}{10}$ $\frac{1}{3}$ $\frac{2}{5}$ $\frac{2}{3}$ $\frac{5}{6}$
d) 0.04 $\frac{1}{3}$ 45% $\frac{1}{2}$ 0.54

5   a) 2   b) 5   c) –2

6

Decimal	Fraction	Percentage
0.3	$\frac{3}{10}$	30
0.25	$\frac{1}{4}$	25
0.6	$\frac{3}{5}$	60

Test your knowledge 2

1   a)

n	1	2	3
White squares, w	3	6	9
Black squares, s	2	2	2
Total squares, t	5	8	11

c)   (i) $3n$ (ii) 2   (iii) $3n + 2$
2   a) $p = 3n + 5$
    b) $p = 4n - 2$
3   a) $4(2 + 6) = 32\,cm^2$
    b) $8(4 + 2) = 48\,cm^2$
4   a) $\frac{1^2}{2} = \frac{1}{2}\,m^2$ b) $\frac{4^2}{2} = 8\,m^2$

5   $p = 6 - q$ ✓
    $p + 6 = q$ ✗
    $p = q - 6$ ✗
    $q = p - 6$ ✗
    $q + p = 6$ ✓
    $6 = q + p$ ✓
    $q - p = 6$ ✗

6   a) $g = \frac{20}{h} = \frac{20}{2} = 10$ b) $h = \frac{20}{g} = \frac{20}{5} = 4$
    c) $h = \frac{20}{g} = \frac{20}{0.1} = 200$

Test your knowledge 3

1   a) $A = b \times h = 5 \times 3 = 15\,cm^2$
        $P = 5 + 3 + 5 + 3 = 16\,cm$
    b) $A = b \times h \div 2 = 8 \times 6 \div 2 = 24\,cm^2$
        $P = 6 + 8 + 10 = 24\,cm$
2   Two possible answers: A 4 by 4 rectangle ($A = P = 16$),
    or a 6 by 3 rectangle ($A = P = 18$)
3   A, H and J
    D, E and F
    C and G
    B doesn't join with any points labelled

4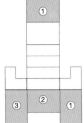

5 a) A (0, 2)   B (4, 2)
  b) There are many answers. Most likely are two from (1, 2), (2, 2), (3, 2). Any answer (x, 2) where x takes any value is correct.
  c) (2, 0) or (2, 4)
6 a) Right-angled triangle   b) Isosceles triangle
  c) Trapezium

Test your knowledge 4

1 a) $\frac{1}{11}$ b) $\frac{7}{11}$ c) 0
2 a) $\frac{12}{20} = \frac{6}{10} = \frac{3}{5}$ b) $\frac{5}{20} = \frac{1}{4}$ c) $\frac{7}{20}$
3   = 13

4 a) 8 ×6   b) 10 ×2

×2

×4

×3

×1

5 a) $465 \times 12 = 465 \times 10 + 465 \times 2 = 4650 + 930 = 5580$
  b) $49 \times 64 = 50 \times 64 - 1 \times 64 = 3200 - 64 = 3136$
6 a) $16 \times 12.5 = 8 \times 25 = 400$
  b) $9 \times 16\frac{1}{3} = 3 \times 49 = 147$

Test your knowledge 5

1 a) F = C + C + 30 or F = 2C + 30
  b) 16 + 16 + 30 = 62°F
  c) 130 = 2C + 30   2C = 100   C = 50
2 a)

		9p + 18		
	3p + 3	3p + 6	3p + 9	
p	p + 1	p + 2	p + 3	p + 4

  b) 36
  c) −1
3 a) 13.2 m = 1320 cm
  b) 6700 mm = 6.7 m
  c) 25 miles ≈ 40 km
  d) 15 ft ≈ 5 m

e) 562 g = 0.562 kg
f) 1250 ml = 1.25 l
4 a) 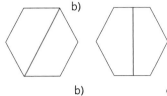   b)

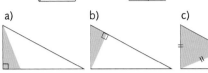

5 a)   b)   c)

Test your knowledge 6

1 a) 12
  b) 16 − 8 = 8
  c) 8 + 16 + 12 = 36
  d) $\frac{8}{36} = \frac{4}{18} = \frac{2}{9}$

2 a) $\frac{90}{360} = \frac{1}{4}$
  b) $\frac{1}{4}$ of 120 = 120 ÷ 4 = 30
  c) $\frac{120}{360} = \frac{1}{3}$. $\frac{1}{3}$ of 120 = 40

3 36 : 48
  18 : **24**
  9 : 12
  3 : **4**
4 2:3 = 5 shares. 30 days ÷ 5 = 6 days per share.
  2 shares = 2 × 6 days = 12 days expected to be rainy.
5 a) 24   b) 24
6 a) 24
  b) 11, or any prime number greater than 10

Test your knowledge 7

1

a	b	c
60°	20°	**100°**
40°	**100°**	40°
35°	25°	**120°**
45°	90°	**45°**
2°	**172°**	6°

2 a = (180 − 70) ÷ 2 = 55°
  b = 180 − 90 − 70 = 20°
3 a)

b) (i)   (ii)

D can be anywhere not on the original lines, and not at C.

4

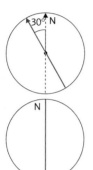

5

6 a)   b)

Test your knowledge 8

1 a) 3
   b) 2
   c) $(0 + 2 + 4 + 6 + x) \div 5 = 4$
      $(0 + 2 + 4 + 6 + x) = 20$
      $x = 8$

2 a) $18 - 12 = 6$
   b) $11 + 6 = 17$, or $13 - 6 = 7$
      i.e. 7 or 17

3 a) $\frac{1}{5} = \frac{2}{10}$. $\frac{2}{10} + \frac{3}{10} = \frac{5}{10} = \frac{1}{2}$
   b) $\frac{3}{4} = \frac{6}{8}$ $\frac{6}{8} - \frac{3}{8} = \frac{3}{8}$

4 $\frac{1}{2}$ of $\frac{1}{2}$ of $\frac{1}{2} = \frac{1}{2} \times \frac{1}{2} \times \frac{1}{2} = \frac{1}{8}$

   i.e. one eighth of the light outside passes through all
   three panes in the window.

5 A $x = -2$
   B $y = -3$
   C $x + y = 4$
   D $y = 2x$

6 a)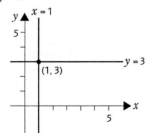

   b) (1, 3)

Test your knowledge 9

1
Input	Output
4	**6**
2	**0**
1	**−3**
−2	**−12**
0	-6

2 The first operation is $\times 4$, the second is −1.

3 a) 150 acres
   b) 20 hectares
   c) $24 \times 2.5 = 60$ acres

4 a)

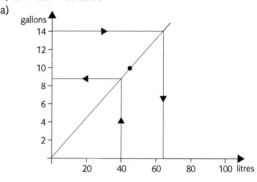

   b) (i)   63 litres
      (ii)   8.8 gallons
      (iii) $8.8 \times 5 = 44$ litres.

5 a) 5

   b)
p	1	2	3	4	5	......	12
t	4	9	14	**19**	**24**		**59**

   c) $t = 5p - 1$

6 a) $2n - 1$
   b) $2n + 1$
   c) $3n - 1$
   d) $3n + 1$